ROLAND V. BINGHAM

The Making of the Beautiful - The Life Story of Annie Johnson Flint

HAYDEN PRESS
PUBLISHING

First published by Hayden Press 2019

Copyright © 2019 by Roland V. Bingham

Roland V. Bingham asserts the moral right to be identified as the author of this work.

Second edition

*This book was professionally typeset on Reedsy.
Find out more at reedsy.com*

Contents

Foreword   iv
Preface   vi
1   The Foregleam   1
2   A Prose Picture of a Poet Written by Herself   5
3   A Christmas Eve Baby   12
4   School Days   16
5   Characteristics   25
6   Mixing the Bitter-Sweet   27
7   Pressed Into Poetry and Print   31
8   The Poetical Theologian   40
9   Songs of Comfort   51
10   Sunset and Eventide   59
More by Annie Johnson Flint   67
More From Hayden Press   69

Foreword

If you ever had the privilege of calling upon Annie Johnson Flint, you would not have forgotten her hands. Anyone who ever saw them, and who had read any of her poems in manuscript, must have marvelled at the clear and beautiful writing which her painfully distorted hands were able to produce. Those instruments of expression which most of us can use so freely, were carefully trained to do their manual work with fine restraint and regularity, and perfect legibility. But this ability to use her physical disabilities far more blessedly than so many of us use our abilities, was seen typically. but not chiefly in such control. It was revealed far more deeply than that in the outpouring of a courageous, chastened, and God-given spirit of glad-hearted service in the name of the Lord whom she loved, and by whose grace her gifts were brought to such abundant fruition.

Annie Johnson Flint's poems were not simply the unskilled utterances of a devout spirit. They disclose by their gracious art, the hand of the true poet who knows that religious verse-writing at its best requires not only a consecrated insight, but lest the message be halted and perhaps lost, a due regard for the most exacting canons in the use of rich and fitting words, musical rhythm, and correct verse forms. Hard work very often lies back of seemingly spontaneous utterances in which these principles of verse writing are followed. Miss Flint was one of the few writers of religious poems in whose work one recognizes in the very ease of it, the hand of the careful artist. There was no distortion in that inward instrument of consecrated expression.

One day a visitor stepped from Miss Flint's sitting room· into the sleeping room to secure a certain reprint of a poem for Miss Flint, who was seated in her wheeled chair. A glance at the bed in that room was revealing. Nine soft pillows were carefully arranged on the bed for use in protecting the exquisitely sensitive, pain-smitten body from the normal contact of the bed-clothing, so distressing it was for her to recline in the hope of rest at night. And it was this most sensitive sufferer who, out of her keen experiences of pain, prepared so many poem pillows for the weary, the suffering, the discouraged in body, mind and spirit. The message of her life is found in just such episodes, and just such lovely, heartening, deeply spiritual poems as are included in this book. Here is an exhibit of what God can do with a life so bound and yet so gloriously free, in a ministry rarely granted to any dweller in our needy world.

Philip E. Howard (1870-1946)
  President of the Sunday School Times Company
  Philadelphia, Pennsylvania

* * *

Preface

Welcome to this biography of Annie Johnson Flint. We trust that you will find it as inspirational as the countless thousands of people have done in the generations before us. If you do, then you will be interested to know that we have recently published three volumes of Annie's poems in both paperback and eBook formats: "He Giveth More Grace", "God Hath Not Promised" and "Grace Sufficient". Each of these would make a wonderful gift to introduce Annie to yet more readers. What we have found is that lovers of Annie's work just cannot wait to share it with others! You can find links to each of these publications at the end of the book.

We are also very excited to let you know about our audiobook of "He Giveth More Grace" with fabulous narration from the Los Angeles actor Abigail Reno. This is now available from all the major online audiobook stores, as well as local libraries for borrowing. We also anticipate producing audiobooks for the remaining material in the near future, so please do look out for them! If you would like to listen to a short sample, you can find it on Soundcloud or you can click on this link.

Finally, if you would like to participate in an online community that celebrates the work of Annie Johnson Flint, and get the opportunity for free Annie-related downloads, then you might wish to like the The Poetry of Annie Johnson Flint Facebook page: https://www.facebook.com/anniejohnsonflint.

1

The Foregleam

Her life, at best, would have been garbed in drab or grey but for the touch of God. Its well-nigh forty years spent as a "shut-in" within the compass of four walls, with the occasional break of an excursion in an invalid chair, would only have attained to one color. And any expression of sound would have been in monotone. In one of her poems she did liken herself to the fern in the flower kingdom, intended with its living green to brighten the shade of the forest. But the highest point her poetic genius could have reached in this realm, would have bestowed on her only a crown of "maidenhair."

But the touch of the Almighty did something more than that for this one: even more than realize the goal of her water-lily song which pictures "The Soul" as climbing from the mud and ooze of the underworld until its white and yellow burst into bloom on the water's brim. We think her life-story is best introduced, as it was surely characterized, by her lovely poem, "The Making of the Beautiful," for God took this life in its colourless shade and sorrow, and touched it with all the hues of the rainbow. And then

He made its monotony burst into tones whose harmonies have blessed the world in their blending of the highest and deepest notes of human experience; "The Making of the Beautiful" gives her early impressions and response to the touch of the Master Hand.

The Making of the Beautiful

Meadow and vale and mountain,
Ocean and lake and wood,
God looked on the fruit of His labor
And saw that His work was good;
And yet was there something lacking
In the world that He had made,
Something to brighten the greenness,
Something to lighten the shade.

He took a shred of the rainbow,
A bit of the sunshine's gold,
The colors of all the jewels
The mines of earth enfold,
A piece of the mist of evening
With the sunset woven through,
A scrap of the sky at noonday,
A clear, unclouded blue;

Of these He fashioned the flowers,
And some were red, like the rose,
And some were a lovely azure,
And some were pale as the snows;
Some, shaped like a fairy chalice

THE FOREGLEAM

The perfumed honey to hold,
And some were stars of silver,
And some were flakes of gold.

They flashed in the gloom of the forests,
They clung to the boughs of the trees,
They hid in the grass of the meadows,
They drifted away on the breeze,
They fell in the clefts of the canyons
And high on the mountains bare,
Where never an eye should see them
Save His Who had made them fair.

But still there was something wanting,
His labor was not yet done;
He gathered more of the colors
Of rainbow and sky and sun,
And now unto these He added
The music of sea and land,
The tune of the rippling river,
The splash of the waves on the sand,

The raindrops' lilting measure,
The pine tree's crooning sigh,
The aspen's lisping murmur,
The wind's low lullaby,
Faint fluting of angel voices
From heavenly courts afar,
And the softest, dreamiest echoes
Of the song of the morning star.

Then deftly His fingers moulded
The strong and the delicate things
Instinct with the joy and the beauty
Of song and of soaring wings;
Nightingale, heron and seagull,
Bobolink, lark-and then,
I think that He smiled a little
As He tilted the tail of the wren,

As He made the owl's face solemn
And twisted the blue jay's crest,
As He bent the beak of the parrot
And smoothed the oriole's vest,
As He burnished the crow's jet plumage
And the robin's breast of red;
"In the cold of the northern springtime
The children will love it," He said.

So some were quaint and cunning,
And some were only frail,
And some He gave a song to,
And lo, the birds of the air.
And the snippets of things left over,
He tossed out under the skies,
Where, falling, fluttering, flying,
Behold, they were butterflies!

2

A Prose Picture of a Poet Written by Herself

Only one prose production of Annie Johnson Flint is extant. Just once she turned from the poet's muse, and it is not strange that even then instead of writing common prose her pen ran from poetry to allegory.

Outside of Bunyan's immortal work, we wonder whether a sweeter picture in allegorical form has ever been drawn. It presents in a fascinating manner a spiritual interpretation of her own life, and breathes the same air of faith and love, and confidence in the guidance and goodness of God that marked all she wrote. It was found among her papers in her own handwriting, with corrections as she had made them, ere laying down her pen. Before presenting her life story it makes a fitting Autobiography as the Allegory of Annie Johnson Flint.

* * *

THE LIFE IN ALLEGORY - "THAT I MIGHT BE LIKE UNTO HIM"

And it came to pass, as I travelled along the Highway of Life, that I saw in the distance, far ahead, a mountain, and on it One standing, upon whose face rested a divine compassion for the grief of the world. His raiment was white and glittering, and in His hand was a cross. And He called unto the sons of men, saying "Come! Come! Who will take up his cross and follow me, that he may be like unto me, and that I may seat him at my right hand and share with him things glorious and beautiful beyond the dreams of earth and the imaginings of men?"

And I said. "What is my cross, that I may take it up?"

And a Voice answered, "There are many crosses, and thine shall be given thee in good time."

And I said, "What will bring me near to Thee and make me most like Thee?"

And the Voice replied, "There are many angels with whom thou canst walk; but see that they lead thee only toward me, and never away from me, for some there be that will cause thee to forget me."

And I said, "What angel shall be given me?"

And I felt a hand laid upon mine, and saw beside me one with a smiling face, who said, "Walk with me: I am the Angel of Joy."

Then all my life grew bright and wealth was mine, and many pleasures, and friends crowded around me, and Love crowned me, and I knew no care.

But suddenly I heard the Voice, and it sounded faint and far-off, and it said, "Alas! Thou art not coming toward me." And I fell upon my knees, crying, " Oh, forgive me that I could forget Thee! Take away the angel since he leads me not unto Thee."

Then the world grew dark and I heard a low voice beside me saying, "Come with me: I am the Angel of Sorrow."

Then he took my hand in his, and I went with him, weeping. But now there were no friends around me, and pleasure palled upon me, and my heart was very sad. And as I went I saw that the Vision grew brighter, and I perceived that I was no longer walking away from it. But my soul was exceeding sorrowful and I looked back often, and saw in memory the joys I had once known, until the tears blinded me, and I stumbled continually, for the path was rough, and it had begun to lead upward.

Then I heard the Voice again, and it said, "Look not back; regret not the past; I will send thee another angel who will help thee to forget the things that are behind."

Then the Sorrowful Angel vanished, and in his place stood one whose face was cheerful. And he said, "Come! Let us be up and doing; I am the Angel of Work."

And I went with him – at first with lagging steps and a sore heart: but as my sight became clearer, I beheld many sick and discouraged, many who had fallen by the way. Then I heard the Voice again saying. "The laborers are few. Inasmuch as ye have done it unto the least of these, ye have done it unto me."

So I began to help those around me, and as my hands grew busy, my heart lightened, and I forgot to look behind me and mourn for the lost joys of the past, and at times there was even a song upon my lips. But the road was rough and often dark, and whiles my courage failed me and my soul was disquieted within me. For there were sorrows I could not comfort, and hunger I could not satisfy, and burdens I could not help to lift. And I could only stretch out my hands, and cry, "Oh, Thou who hast helped me, help these, for I cannot."

Then the Voice said, "Be not weary in well-doing. Thou art

coming toward me. I will send one who will bring thee still nearer."

Then I saw beside me an angel with a veil before his face, who said in a grave voice, "Canst thou walk with me? I am the Angel of Sacrifice."

But I shrank back, murmuring, "What wilt thou take from me ?" And he answered, "I will take nothing. Thou must thyself give it of thine own free will. It is thy Dearest Wish."

"Then I hid my face in my hands, and cried, "I cannot! I cannot! Ask me something else ! Give me some task to do ! Have I not labored faithfully these many days? Did I not myself resign the joys that were once so precious to me, and turn away from them to follow Thee ? And I will still follow Thee - still work for Thee, only leave me this one thing! It is so dear to me - it is my light in darkness, my food in hunger, my rest in weariness, my comfort always. And yet I have not loved it better than Thee: it has not led me away from Thee, nor hidden from me the Heavenly Vision."

Then the Voice said, "Thou canst do without all these things - light and food, rest and comfort, but canst thou do without me? And thou must choose between us. Is it too hard for thee? And yet thou saidst thou wouldst be nearer me!"

Then I cried in answer, "Yes, yes, I would; but Oh! Is there not another way ? Take all else, and leave me only this!" But the Voice spoke no more.

Then I struggled until the sweat broke out upon my brow in drops of agony, and my nights were sleepless, and my days troubled, and the Vision grew dim, and I saw no light.

But then came a day when the Higher triumphed, and with broken voice and streaming eyes, I held out my Dearest Wish, crying, "Take it, take it! Thy will be done!"

Then the Vision broke in splendor, and I heard the Voice saying, "Thou hast fought a good fight. Now thou art indeed mine: and behold thy reward is even now beside thee."

So I looked, and the angel had lifted his veil and was smiling, and lo! it was the Wish I had given up, but changed – beautified and glorified, a heavenly blessing in the place of an earthly. Then it vanished from my sight, and the Voice spoke again: "Thy sacrifice is accepted. Thou shalt see· it no more on Earth; but through all the days of thy mortal pilgrimage it shall be to thee a blessed hope, and it shall meet thee at the gate of Heaven, to be thine through all eternity. And thou hast come much nearer unto me, and art more like me. Dost thou desire to draw still nearer to me?"

And I cried, "Yes, yes, still nearer !" And the Voice replied, "There is but one angel more for thee to walk with. It is the Angel of Suffering."

Then a great trembling seized me and I said, "The spirit is willing, but the flesh is weak. I know not if I can endure. Yet do with me as Thou wilt, for I am Thine."

Then suddenly there appeared before me an angel whose face was lined and furrowed as with the deep strokes of a chisel, yet over all there was the beauty of a conquered peace – a peace wrested from great tribulation, the look of one who had forgotten how to weep. And one hand he held out to me, and with the other he pointed to the ground. And I looked and saw before me the cross which I had last seen in the hand of Him upon the Mount.

Then the Voice said, "This only is the way by which thou canst approach nearest unto me and be most like me. This is thy cross. Lie down upon it without shrinking and without fear. Thou shalt not be alone: I too have been there. I sounded all the depths of pain, and at the last I was forsaken by the Father; but that last, worst suffering thou shalt not know, for I will never leave thee nor forsake thee."

So I lay down upon the cross, and I rest upon it even unto this day. And the Angel of Suffering watches upon my left hand, and upon my right is one who comes always with him ... the Angel of His Presence. And of late there has been another, the Angel of Peace. And the three abide always with me.

And the Vision is a Vision no longer, but a Reality. And it is not a stern Judge, nor a merciful God, but a loving Father, who bends over me. The way has brought me almost to His feet. There is but a narrow valley that divides us, the Valley of the Shadow, and the angel who shall lead me through it is the Angel of Death. I wait his coming with a tranquil heart, for beneath the mask that frights the timid human hearts which dread his summons I shall see a face I know - the face of the Son of God, who has walked beside me in the furnace of affliction, so that I passed through without even the smell of fire on my garments.

And when I go down into the deep waters, it is His arm I shall lean upon, and the voice that welcomes me upon the other side will be His. And from the bank of the river the path leads upward to the City, which hath foundations, whose builder and maker is God, and they that enter in shall go no more out forever. And at the gate my Guide shall leave me, and I shall see Him no more until I behold Him at the right hand of God, having upon His head many crowns, and on His vesture a name written, "King of Kings, and Lord of Lords", before whose face heaven and earth shall flee away.

And the nations of them that are saved shall stand before Him, and they that come up out of great tribulation, who endure unto the end, and inherit all things, and they shall cry with a loud voice saying, "Blessing and honor and glory and power be unto Him that sitteth upon the throne, and unto the Lamb for ever and ever."

And in Him who sitteth upon the throne I shall know the Man of Sorrows, Whom I saw upon the Mount of the Vision, holding in His hand a cross and calling unto the sons of men, "Come! Come! Who will take up his cross and follow me, that he may be like unto me, and that I may seat him upon my right hand, and share with him things glorious and beautiful beyond the dreams of earth and the imaginings of men?"

3

A Christmas Eve Baby

In spite of the adage that poets are born and not made, we do not fancy there was anything more rhythmic in the cry that ushered Annie Johnson Flint into this world, than that which marked the advent of any other child: and yet it does seem strange that this one who was to become one of America's great poets should have been born on the eve when, long centuries before, the angels had first heralded their song of joy concerning the coming Saviour.

Annie was born on Christmas Eve, in the year 1866, in the little town of Vineland, New Jersey. Was it this that made her pen long years after run so sweetly in her Christmas verses? Did the baby catch the angel carols that night that Eldon and Jean Johnson, the father and mother, welcomed that Christmas present as the greatest earthly gift? The father was of English descent, while the mother claimed that she was Scotch. (A funny thing happened a few months before Miss Flint's death. A Spiritualist wrote that he had had an interview with this mother in the spirit world, and proceeded to give a description that had not an atom of truth in it - but the "spirit" made a last guess in saying she was "Scotch"). But the only remembrance of that mother dates back to the time just before the tragedy which was to rob her forever of that mother's care. She was ushered in, a little three-year-old tot, to the room where her mother was lying, and introduced to a newly arrived baby sister. She must have looked with wonder from that baby face into the mother's face that day, for it is the one and only imprint of that mother's likeness that lives in memory.

It was indelible. The baby was left for life-long companionship, and still remains, but the mother shortly after this episode was taken from her forever. When, at the early age of twenty-three, that mother passed away, the father took the children to board with the widow of an old army comrade who had been killed in the Civil War. It was not a happy arrangement. The woman had two children of her own and her means were very limited. During the two years the Johnson girls added to the cares of that family; they were most evidently unwelcome and unwanted. But it was at this time, when the outlook seemed so dark for their young lives, that a neighbor interposed in a kindly way. She looms in Miss Flint's memory as 'Aunt Susie', although she could claim no blood relationship to this friend.

Aunt Susie was a school teacher, and boarded near the school in the home of Mr. and Mrs. Flint. She became so strongly attached to the Johnson girls that she was continually speaking of them to the Flints, and at last so aroused their sympathy on behalf of the motherless children, that a little over two years after their mother's death they were adopted by Mr. and Mrs. Flint, whose name from henceforth they bore. While their name might sound hard and stony, their hearts were very tender. Two things made Mr. Johnson willing to part with the children: first, he was suffering at the time with an incurable disease from which he shortly afterwards died; then, the Flints offered a home after his own desire and thought for the children, as they were Baptists, and Mr. Johnson was very anxious that the children should be brought up in the Baptist faith, as he was a strong believer himself in their position.

But God had higher thoughts than that this one should be simply pressed into the Baptist mould. It was in His plan that, like John Bunyan, her pen should bless the whole household of faith. Later she was converted in a Methodist revival meeting, and many of her most intimate friends were connected with that church. Then as the years rolled by she was helped by men and women in all branches of the evangelical church, and in return she herself became God's channel of blessing to that wider fellowship. She looked upon that "household of faith" as really one great family, with one faith, one Lord, one baptism, working under one Divine Spirit, having one Master over all.

Mr. and Mrs. Flint were true Christians, and love reigned in their home. The two girls were taken right to their hearts, and loved as though they were their own flesh and blood. The daily training was thorough, both in the Christian and the domestic sphere. When Annie was eight years old the family left the farm and moved into Vineland, New Jersey, but the touch of that country life never left her in all the after years. When they reached their new home in town, revival meetings were in progress, and she attended. It was during one of these meetings that the Spirit of God operated upon that young heart and brought her to saving faith in Christ.

She always believed that at that time she was truly converted, and while she did not join the church until ten years later, she never doubted that the eternal work was then wrought. She strongly deprecated the idea that young children cannot apprehend spiritual truths. She felt that the divine mysteries were often plainer to the simple faith of a child than to many adults, blinded by their own prejudices and intellectual doubts. It was not difficult for her to endorse the words of the Master, "Thou hast hidden these things from the wise and prudent, and hast revealed them unto babes."

4

School Days

It was about the time that she passed through this spiritual experience that the poetic muse began to awaken within her. She tells of the thrill of her life when she realized that she could express herself in verse. Then came another move. When she was fourteen the family went to Camden, New Jersey, and there the two girls continued their schooling. There was nothing special to mark the years that flew by in that time. She was very fond of reading, and made good use of her adopted father's library, which contained a goodly number of the works of standard authors, such as Scott, Dickens, Kingsley, and Bulwer Lytton, in addition to the majority of the poets.

It was at this period that she formed one friendship that continued through the years. This girl friend tells of her early recollections of Annie as she then appeared, "a pretty, dark-eyed girl, with a clear olive complexion, and long black curls. She was kind-hearted, merry and vivacious - a general favourite with the boys and girls at school." This friend writes, "We sat together at school, whenever the teacher permitted it. We were both very fond of reading. Well do I remember the day when we read 'Madcap Violet' in school. We kept up the absorbed, studious look for the occasion, while that delightful novel was safely hidden behind the friendly covers of Swinton's Geography. We had much in common," says this girl friend. "Every Saturday afternoon we met, a select literary society of two, to read our favourite poets, and then we attempted verse ourselves. Annie wrote one poem which I greatly admired. It began something like this:

> "A white-robed star was dressed for the stage
> But still she glanced at the printed page.
> Mother! It was years since she had seen her face,
> And now she was dead, and the dear old place
> Was in strange hands."

The ending was tragic - amusingly so, as one sees it today. It continued:

> "And there in the solemn twilight,
> There in the silvery moonlight,
> There with outstretched arms she lay, ·
> Waiting for the break of day.
> There in the morning they found her,
> With white robes glimmering round her,
> With arms stretched wildly above her head
> There on the eve of her triumph - dead."

Not to be outdone in this, this friend wrote several pathetic stanzas describing a gallant ship which finally plunged beneath the waves with all on board. But we are quite sure that Annie's poems were not all tragedy. There was too deep a streak of natural humour with her to exclude the comedy. We almost think that it was a reversion to these girlhood school days that drew from her in later years one of her nature songs. She entitled it, "How to Tell a Comet." You might almost think that she was sitting in the old school when she penned the lines, with the sub-title, "Astronomy Made Easy." It went as follows:

> Though you may not know a planet
> From a bird that's called a gannet,
> Nor distinguish Sagittarius from Mars;
> Though the beasts in that strange zoo
> May all look alike to you,
> And you lump the whole caboodle just as 'stars';
> Though you cannot place the Lion,
> Nor correctly trace Orion,
> Nor discern the jewelled belt he proudly wears,
> Nor the Big and Little Hounds,
> Through those happy hunting grounds,
> Nightly chasing up the Big and Little Bears;
> Though you cannot tell the Dipper
> From your grandpa's old felt slipper,
> And to name the constellations you would fail,
> There's one thing that you may know
> And be very sure it's so,
> You can always tell a comet by its tail.
> Its airy, hairy, winking, blinking, flowing, glowing tail;
> Its fiery, wiry, gleaming, streaming, flaring, glaring tail.

Then this girlhood friend says, "There came a time of the usual writing of love stories. For one of these the teacher who discovered it called the unfortunate author to stay after school. She confiscated Annie's most brilliant attempt and gave her a severe lecture. 'I didn't suppose any one of my pupils knew enough about love to write a grown-up, sensational love story', she said in a shocked voice." When this friend moved from Annie's home to another town, we know little of her later companionships. These two kept in touch to the close of life.

These years were the formative years. It was then she became more conscious of herself as an individual and of her surroundings. She realized, too, her good fortune in having such a home and such foster parents. The Flints were people of high principle. They taught the girl to be self-reliant, independent and economical. They gave her a healthy horror of debt. "Owe no man anything," was a command tacitly obeyed. In those days there was no buying on the installment plan. If one had the money to purchase, then the article wanted was secured, otherwise one went without. Then, she acquired a very hearty contempt for what she called the "leaners in life" - the shiftless mortals who allow others to bear their burdens and pay their way, and make no effort themselves to better their condition. She had no use for those who spent their time in pitying themselves.

Their parents provided a good home with plenty to eat and enough to wear, but there was no waste. "Gather up the fragments that nothing be lost" was a rule strictly observed. By this time she made all her own clothes as well as her mother's, except their best dresses, for which a dressmaker came into the house twice a year. She was also capable of taking charge of the housekeeping if necessary. One thing that is apparent from these earliest years is that she was a keen observer whether she was in the country or in the city. It was these early observations on the Jersey Coast that in later years she turned so beautifully and helpfully into poetic language under the title, "The Set of the Sail."

> I stood on the shore beside the sea;
> The wind from the West blew fresh and free,
> While past the rocks at the harbor's mouth
> The ships went North and the ships went South,
> And some sailed out on an unknown quest,
> And some sailed in to the harbor's rest;
> Yet ever the wind blew out of the West.
> I said to one who had sailed the sea
> That this was a marvel unto me;
> For how can the ships go safely forth,
> Some to the South and some to the North,
> Far out to sea on their golden quest,
> Or in to the harbor's calm and rest,
> And ever the wind blow out of the West?
> The sailor smiled as he answered me,
> 'Go where you will when you're on the sea,
> Though head winds baffle and flaws delay,
> You can keep the course by night and day,
> Drive with the breeze or against the gale;
> It will not matter what winds prevail,
> For all depends on the set of the sail.'

Then in the other verses of this poem she makes the application. Of course the moralizing came in the later years. This keen observation of everything in nature comes out in one of the earlier booklets published, entitled, "Out of Doors." We think it is Nature's poetic classic. Take a verse out of her poem entitled "The Creator':

> He takes the scent of the softening ground
> Where the first green blade pricks through,
> He takes the reddening maple bough
> A-slant against the blue,
> He takes the cheer in the robin's song
> And the flash of the blue-bird's wing,
> The joy of prisoned things set free,
> And of these He makes the Spring.

Follow on with the next verse:

> He takes the sheen of the waving wheat
> Where the slow cloud-shadows pass,
> He takes the brook's soft rippling tune
> And the daisied meadow grass,
> He takes the swish of the mower's scythe
> In the noontide's hot, white glare,
> The joy of labor and growing things,
> And makes the Summer fair.

That poem will remain a masterpiece ...

It was in the girlhood years that there was stored up in the child mind the wealth of these things that burst forth in the later years. In those long, long years in which she was "shut in" those nature psalms would never have had the touch that was given to them but for the memories of girlhood when she ran untrammelled under Heaven's canopy and out into the open fields and woods. Not that she lost her observation of nature! I remember standing beside her sick couch one day when she suddenly observed, "We are going to have rain today. My robin has just changed his note. He never sings in that tone unless the rain is coming." Sure enough, the rain came. When she wrote that sweet song. "The Lullaby of Rain," one finds there the blending of girlhood impressions gleaned in city and country. Intermingled also is seen the struggle with life's difficulties that marked her later days. And yet it too is a classic. It commences with the words:

"Through the sultry city daylight I had toiled with throbbing head,
But at night, though spent and weary, slumber from my wooing fled;
Still before my aching vision lines of figures came and went,
Ghosts of those long hours of labor and the day's imprisonment.
Only glare and tumult entered through the window opened wide,
Naught of freshness e'er could reach me from the surging human tide;
Then, a muttered growl of thunder and the lightning's far-off flare,
And a sudden breath of coolness in the hot and murky air;
There's a patter on the shingles and a tap against the pane,
Oh, the orchestra is tuning for the Lullaby of Rain!"

As we read on through that poem we pass from the sultry heat of summer, the weariness and burden of the sweltering day, right into the beauty and refreshment of the thunderstorm that bursts and the shower that follows. Clear through to the close the muse is on her, and she carries you right on with her. Listen:

> I can hear the sleepy twitter of a bird's note from the trees,
> And the meadow-brook's hoarse murmur, borne upon the rising breeze;
> There's a choked and chuckling gurgle from the overflowing eaves,
> And a drip! drip! drip! staccato from the soaked and streaming leaves,
> Then a rush along the shingles and a dash against the pane.
> Oh, a hundred voices mingle in the Lullaby of Rain!
> Now the single sounds are merging in a crescendo roar
> That shall drown all lesser noises in its pelting pour;
> Hence, ye phantoms of old labor! ye shall haunt me now in vain
> As I drift away to dreamland to the Lullaby of Rain.

But perhaps the results of her girlhood rambles in the Jersey woods and along the Jersey coast was never brought out better in the later years than in her two poems: "From Forest to Fender" and "Nature's Shut-Ins." In the latter she likens the shut-in life to the ferns in God's flower kingdom, always found in the shade and cool retreats, in their greatest beauty when most hidden. Those two poems reached a shut-in lady in the Middle States. She was deeply touched and moved by them. She had not Miss Flint's gift of poetry, but she had the artist's eye and the artist's touch. She was lying on her back year after year and her one occupation was with the artist's brush. She had them fasten her paper on a canvas over her bed and lying there she did most exquisite paintings.

She took these two poems and verse by verse she put the artist's touch in the margin. The flowers to which Miss Flint referred were all painted in in their natural colours, beautifully done, and then she sent the book, with its hand-painted touch, to Miss Flint as a tribute of one shut-in to another. Miss Flint prized these two poems so wonderfully illustrated as a precious treasure.

5

Characteristics

Whether by nature or through her early Christian experience, Miss Flint was generally disposed to be cheerful and optimistic. She looked on the bright side of life, and was quite fond of jokes and able to get as much enjoyment out of life as possible. Aunt Susie had often told her that when she was just learning to walk she marched across the room with head up, regardless of any obstacles in the way, and that forward-looking lift of the head was a characteristic attitude. It was typical of the courage which she was to manifest in later life when she was hemmed in by so many trials. She certainly learned to endure hardness as a good soldier of Jesus Christ.

Then she had a generous nature, and was ever ready to share what she had with others, and ever more willing to grant favours than to accept them. But we are sure that it is a mistake to touch on the commendable characteristics in her life records without lifting the veil on the other side. Annie was very human, and she herself had left a record of the glaring faults as she saw them. While still a child she had a very quick temper which flared up on slight provocation, but as quickly died down. She never claimed entire freedom from this tendency, but she had learned the secret of grace in overcoming.

Another characteristic was her acute sensitiveness, which made her keenly alive to the needs and the wrongs of others, and, as is usual with one of this nature, her likes and dislikes were intense. She admits further that if she was accused of something she had not done and for which she was unjustly reproved, she indulged in sulky spells which lasted far longer than the storm of temper. She would not speak to anyone while in these moods nor condescend to explain any mistake which might have been made. This was an unfortunate trait in girlhood.

But she records her greatest fault as lack of patience, with herself as well as with others. She did not like to wait for things. She wanted to see results at once. With this there was coupled a dogged persistence and she refused to give up anything once begun, until it was finished. This helped her to accomplish many a hard and distasteful task, but all through her life the hardest lesson she had to learn was patience. Again and again she had to be reminded to wait patiently for the Lord. It was so much easier to wait eagerly and impatiently, or to spend the time making plans and devising schemes for doing something when the waiting time was over. One text that seemed especially written for her was, "Through faith and patience we inherit the promises."

6

Mixing the Bitter-Sweet

F inishing her high school she spent one year at normal and then had a position offered to her. It was a great temptation to begin earning money, and as her mother was failing in health, and had had one slight stroke, she felt that she was really needed at home, so she started teaching the primary class in the same school that she had attended as a girl. According to her contract with the normal school she taught for three years, though early in the second year arthritis showed itself. She tried several doctors in turn, but it steadily grew worse until it became difficult for her to walk at all, and she had hard work to finish out the third year. After that she was obliged to give up her work, and there followed three years of increasing helplessness.

The death of both her adopted parents within a few months of each other left the two girls again alone. There was little money in the bank and the twice-orphaned children had come to a real "Red Sea Place" in their lives. It was just then that the faithful Aunt Susie again came to the rescue. She had been in the Sanitarium at Clifton Springs and was convinced that Annie could find help and healing there. Accordingly, arrangements were made for Miss Flint to go and she was to have the rent of the house she was leaving for her income.

Picture if you can the hopelessness of Miss Flint's position when she finally received the verdict of the doctors of the Clifton Springs Sanitarium that henceforth she would be a helpless invalid. Her own parents had been taken from her in childhood, and then her foster parents both passed away. Her one sister was all too frail and struggling to meet her own situation bravely. Miss Flint was in a condition where she was compelled to be dependent upon the care of others who could not afford to minister to her except as compensated by her. In after years she always stated that her poems were born of the need of others and not from her own need; but one knows full well that she never could have written as she did for the comfort and help of thousands of others if she had not had the background of facing those very crises in her own life.

She tells, for instance, of the circumstances that drew forth that which perhaps has become her most widely known poem, "At the Place of the Sea." A friend wrote her that she was in great difficulty and facing great trouble, and she did not see where she was going to turn for help or what she was going to do. She wished that Miss Flint would help her pray for a way out. She had come to what she termed "the Red Sea place in her life." This expression struck Miss Flint, and she looked up the incident in the Bible. The thing that impressed her most was that though the Israelites did face the Red Sea, and had come to a place of impassable difficulty, where there actually was no way out, yet when God's time came He said to Moses, "Speak unto the children of Israel that they go forward," and when He said go forward, He opened the way.

So she came to write the poem for her friend. She reminded her that the Red Sea was the place where the Lord showed His power in spite of seemingly impassable obstacles. Later this friend wrote saying, with a veritable triumph of Miriam's song in her letter, that the Lord had opened and the Lord led her through. But Miss Flint could never have entered into those conditions had she not been "led through." She would never have been able to help others if she had not passed along the road herself. And so we still feel that what is commonly known as her "Red Sea poem" was born out of her own steps of faith. How could she have met the doubt in other lives if faith had not triumphed in the same sphere for herself? No, that first verse of her poem was beaten out in the bitter experiences of her own life as she wrote to others:

> Have you come to the Red Sea place in your life,
> Where in spite of all you can do
> There is no way out, there is no way back,
> There is no other way but through?
> Then wait on the Lord with a trust serene
> Till the night of your fear is gone;
> He will send the wind, He will heap the floods,
> When He says to your soul, 'Go on.'

And when she went on to say:

> "His hand will lead you through – clear through

> Ere the watery walls roll down."

She knew. She had passed through that way. It was thus that God guided this life into its channel of useful service. She loved music. She had spent much time in seeking to make herself proficient to fill any position in that sphere, and then the disease twisted up those poor fingers, and made playing impossible. It literally drove her to write poems.

7

Pressed Into Poetry and Print

With a pen pushed through bent fingers and held by swollen joints, she wrote first without any thought that it might be an avenue of ministry, or that it would bring her returns that might help her in her support. Her verses provided a solace for her in the long hours of suffering. But then she began the making of hand-lettered cards and gift books, and decorated some of her own verses. Her "Christmas Carols" became popular. Two card publishers printed these greetings, and this helped her to get her foot on the first rung of the ladder of support. It gave her the larger vision of possibly securing openings through some of the magazines, by which her poems could be a wider blessing, and at the same time bring some little return that would minister to her own pressing need.

When we met her first, twenty years ago, she had succeeded in thus placing a number of her poems in the old Christian Endeavour World, and the Sunday School Times had accepted several. From the first her writings appealed to us, and ·we early made them a special feature in the columns of The Evangelical Christian. Testimonies came in from many directions of blessing received, and in 1919 we ventured to put forth the first little brochure of her poems under the title of "By the Way, Travelogues of Cheer."

Miss Flint entered into every detail of the publishing of that first little book of poems with wonderful interest. She was anxious not only as to the poetry, but as to the artistic presentation. She was delighted when the late Rev. W. H. Griffith-Thomas undertook to write the introduction. It proved a marked success and continues to this day one of the most popular of her booklets. Seven of these brochures, ever increasingly attractive, and ever more widely circulated, have now been issued. While her Canadian publishers really "discovered" her, to the Sunday School Times we think she was indebted for the largest step into the widest fellowship. In 1926 the Editors of that paper published a short article setting forth a few facts regarding the songwriter. To the large majority it evidently came as a complete surprise to know that Miss Flint was a shut-in. As soon as that fact became known, and that her support depended largely upon the sale of her books, there came a perfect deluge of letters - no less than three thousand being received in the short space of seven weeks. For the time being she was certainly the best known person in Clifton Springs.

While of course the first response was never repeated, there was the continuance of friendships created. Such spontaneous expressions of goodwill and interest came as a great encouragement to the invalid poetess, and inspired to new efforts to express in song the love and convictions of her heart and life. The issuance of her booklets and the action of the Sunday School

Times linked her up with a world-wide fellowship. For a long time she sought to deal with this ministry herself, and to carry the burden of correspondence. One wonders how she could ever get a pen through those poor twisted fingers; but she was a beautiful writer, and a wonderful correspondent. Her letters were unique, bright and breezy, though written from her bed of affliction. They were as rich as her poems, and whatever the stage of her affliction, or however great the pain through which she might be passing, she always had a touch of humour that was refreshing.

One of her great regrets in the after years was that the progress of her affliction made it necessary to dictate her messages to her friends, and of course this added to her expense. When she could afford it, she liked to go into the Sanitarium for a month or two around the Christmas season. It gave her a little more care and helpful medical treatment and at the same time she came into contact with a large number of guests in that great institution who purchased her booklets and her cards. One of the lessons which she had to learn in connection with the faith life was that she could not dictate to the Lord as to how He was to supply the need. She had been brought up with sturdy independence. She still struggled to make ends meet. She still sought to cut down expenses in order that she might be able to pay as she went. The thought of charity was obnoxious to her. She loved to give to others and help those who were in need, but to receive from others – that was quite another matter.

The breaking down of her prejudice in this sphere came about in a very simple way. One of the boarders staying at the home where she lived, when saying good-bye, tactfully slipped into her hand a gift of money. This was the first time such a thing had ever happened, and Miss Flint's pride was up in arms at once. The woman evidently noticed a difference in her manner and explained she wished to leave some remembrance with her but, not knowing what Miss Flint's special need might be, thought it better to let her choose. Then she added something which went home. Miss Flint never forgot it. She said, "You know Jesus Christ said, 'It is more blessed to give than to receive.' But how can there be any givers to whom the blessing can come unless there are those who are willing to receive? It takes two halves to make a whole."

Then she appealed to Miss Flint and asked if their positions were reversed, and she had the means would she not be glad to give? This turned things around so completely that Miss Flint had to own that she had no right to withhold the blessing of giving from others. She took the gift so kindly meant, and tried to be a willing receiver if that would help some giver to obtain a blessing. Her life was lived, as someone has said, from hand to mouth, but as she liked to have it expressed, the mouth was hers, and the hand was God's, and His hand was never empty.

But there came times of real trial and testing. Sales sometimes fell off, and extra needs pressed in. Sometimes for considerable periods she had to have a trained nurse. There were doctor's bills running up and then too she was under pressure of many other trials; but again it was in these very conditions that some of the heart experiences wrought by them brought her where she could be a blessing and help to others. One of her sweetest sonnets, which she says was born of the experience of another, would never have found expression if it had not been for her own trials. The special incident that drew it forth was the visit of a little, tired and discouraged deaconess to Clifton Springs. She used to call and tell her troubles to Miss Flint, and when she left and went back to the West, she wrote saying how blue she felt, and how down-hearted, and she didn't see why God allowed such hard things to come into her life. Miss Flint put her answer into a poem. Nothing ever sweeter ever came from her pen. She entitled it, "What God Hath Promised."

> God hath not promised skies always blue,
> Flower strewn pathways all our lives through;
> God hath not promised sun without rain,
> Joy without sorrow, peace without pain.
>
> But God hath promised strength for the day,
> Rest for the labor, light for the way,
> Grace for the trials, help from above,
> Unfailing sympathy, undying love.

We were interested in finding this poem had passed over to Britain. A publisher there sent it to Germany to be brought out in beautiful coloured form. It was most artistically produced, but they had omitted the name of the author. We fancy it became one of the best-selling cards of the British publishers, but at least a share of the profits ought to have gone to maintain the one in whose dark hours triumphant faith had found expression in these words.

Following the example of The Sunday School Times, The Evangelical Christian published a brief sketch of her life. This was done at a time of particular difficulty in Miss Flint's life, and had very blessed results. It was suggested to the constituency of the magazine that if anyone cared to show his or her appreciation of this singer of sweet songs their gifts would be forwarded to Miss Flint. Knowing her extreme sensitiveness on this point, the news of what had been done was conveyed to her very tactfully, and was received with the same unwavering trust in God and implicit faith in His overshadowing providence in her life. The expenses of the invalid had increased greatly and the response to the appeal was gratifying.

For a long time after her need was made known donations came in, until well over $1,000 had been passed on to her to meet the ever-increasing expenses which she had to face owing to the progress of the disease. With the publication of other of her booklets the royalties increased and contributed materially to the supplying of her temporal needs until the time of her death. All of which was a matter of profound thanksgiving with the poetess, to whom Jehovah Jireh, the Lord who supplied, was a present reality.

In another sphere her friends criticized and challenged her faith. As her story became known far and wide it was natural that she should receive many visitors. Many of these were, of course, earnest Christians, and sincerely interested in her welfare. Among them were some who strongly believed that healing of the body was for every child of God. Their claim was that healing was in the Atonement and purchased for us by Christ, and that everyone who was walking obediently could claim deliverance from physical infirmities and bodily sickness. She listened to what they had to say. More than that, she went earnestly and prayerfully to search the Scriptures as to God's will. It was only after most painstaking study and prayer, and the reading of the best writers on this subject, that she reached the conclusion that, while God can and does heal in this way in some cases, in others He does not; that He has seen fit to leave some of the most triumphant saints deeply afflicted.

She saw too that many of those who pressed their theory were themselves compassed with infirmity, and while telling others that they ought to claim healing, bore in their own lives the failure of their theory. Miss Flint became thoroughly convinced that God intended to glorify Himself through her, in her weak, earthen vessel, and while like Paul she had three times, and more, prayed that this might be taken from her, there came to her with real assurance the voice which said, "My grace is sufficient for thee. My strength is made perfect in weakness." She reached the place where she too could say with Paul, "Most gladly, therefore, will I rather glory in my infirmities that the power of Christ may rest upon me."

The faith life always brings faith fellowships, and in her friendships Miss Flint was singularly blessed. She felt that she had been enriched through them, and from all parts of the world she received words that were a constant comfort and stimulation to her. Many of these friends she never saw, and will wait to see them over on the other side. Some of them that she loved dearly went on before her. Perhaps to these we owe the sweet little verse included in her "Songs of Faith and Comfort", and entitled "The Blessings That Remain". The first stanza reads:

> "There are loved ones who are missing
>   From the fireside and the feast;

> There are faces that have vanished,
> There are voices that have ceased;
> But we know they passed forever
> From our mortal grief and pain,
> And we thank Thee, O our Father,
> For the blessings that remain."

It was on one of these occasions when her little group of friends had been visited with sorrow, and when a missionary from South America was mourning the loss of his beloved wife that he sent to Miss Flint a little card on which were printed the words, "I don't look back. The Lord knows all the shortcomings. I don't look in, or I should be wretched. I just keep looking up into His face." It was this that drew from Miss Flint the sweet response in poetic form, "But We See Jesus."

> I don't look back, God knows the fruitless efforts,
> The wasted hours, the sinning, the regrets,
> I leave them all with Him who blots the record,
> And mercifully forgives, and then forgets.
>
> I don't look forward, God sees all the future,
> The road that, short or long, will lead me home,
> And He will face with me its every trial,
> And bear for me the burdens that may come.
>
> But I look up, into the face of Jesus,
> For there my heart can rest, my fears are stilled,
> And there is joy, and love, and light for darkness,
> And perfect peace, and every hope fulfilled.

One of the amusing things about this poem was that when it was published in The Evangelical Christian a lady down south wrote to the Editor saying that a mistake had been made, that her uncle was the author of the poem and that she had found it in his own hand-writing on his desk after his death. This letter was sent to Miss Flint asking for an explanation to satisfy the lady. She remembered perfectly where and why it was written. She remembered also that a few years before she had received a letter from a man in the south. He told her he had read that poem and liked it so much that he wanted to improve it a little. He had gone to the extent of re-writing some of the lines. Not only this, he had printed some copies signing Miss Flint's name, and adding, "Revised by So-and-So." She put his letter aside to answer later when she had cooled off a little, but it was mislaid and could not be found until it turned up in a box of old letters several years afterwards. This identified the uncle and vindicated the author.

8

The Poetical Theologian

There is no place where the Christian has been more orthodox than in his hymn book. It is true that there is occasionally a hymn that is open to criticism by the strict theologian, but as a whole our hymn books have been orthodox and hymns express not only the highest ecstasy of the heart, but the deepest truths of the Scriptures. When one comes to study this life from the theological standpoint it bears out the old idea that religion primarily is of the heart rather than the intellect. With the poet the heart predominates, and in hymnology we have the highest expression of the Christian soul when related aright to Christian truths.

Commencing with God's revelation in Nature, nothing could be better outside of the 19th Psalm and other Scriptures than Annie Johnson Flint's tribute to the Creator as seen in His creation. A poem entitled "The Song of Creation" is classical in its language and rich in its incitement to worship and praise. Some of these would be suitable for expressions of thanksgiving in the great congregation. Another one of these is the "Spring Song of

Praise."

> Praise the Lord, ye heaven of heavens,
> Sun and moon and stars of light;
> Praise Him, all His vast creation,
> Deepest deep and highest height.
> Praise Him, meadow, mount and valley,
> Praise Him, forest, field and stream,
> Praise Him, sky and earth and ocean,
> Roused from ·winter's chilling dream

In most of the dissertations on theology it is customary to commence with the attitude of the writer toward the Scriptures themselves. In this Annie Johnson Flint did more than rhyme out her reasons why she believed the Bible to be the Word of God. In one of her poems, "The Things That Remain," she says:

> And though the little hills shall melt,
> The mighty mountains move,
> Though earth and heaven shall pass away,
> And suns unstable prove,
> Though faithless stars shall cease to shine,
> And there is no more sea,
> Still changeless as the changeless God
> The Word of God shall be.

In another poem on "The Steering Star," she concludes:

> Oh, wavering lights of man's device,
> Oh, burned-out suns of human thought,
> Your fitful gleams will not suffice

> To find the heaven that we sought,
> Light of the world, our hope is here;
> Star of our faith, we look to Thee;
> Sure Word of God, unwavering, clear,
> Guide Thou our souls across the sea.

That strength of conviction in the Word perhaps is never better expressed than in her little poem entitled "I Know." The first verse runs as follows:

> I know - against this fortress wall
> The gates of hell shall not prevail,
> I know in Whom I have believed
> And that His Word shall never fail;
> I know that He is able still,
> Is strong to save and strong to keep.
> And all that I commit to Him
> Is safe, though I may wake or sleep.

But she had no sympathy with those who made great profession of believing the whole Bible and yet were constantly manifesting a spirit contrary to all its deepest teaching. Her thought of the Bible was to have it transferred into the life that it transfigures. In one of her poems on "The World's Bible", she says:

> We are the only Bible
> The careless world will read,
> We are the sinner's gospel,
> We are the scoffer's creed,
> We are the Lord's last message,
> Given in deed and word.

> What if the type is crooked?
> What if the print be blurred?

She felt we were to be living epistles if we were to commend the Gospel which we preach. With the teaching that undermines faith in the Bible under the specious pretext of modern thought she had no sympathy. She saw through its proud claims of superior scholarship, and she paid her respects to them in several of her poems.

But orthodoxy finds its vital test when one comes to the Atonement and the Christ that died. Her little booklet, "Songs of the Saviour", sets forth her position here. Perhaps one of the sweetest in this sphere is the one in which she brings before us the unbelief of Thomas, and his assertion that he would not believe except he could put his fingers in the print of the nails. She says:

> Except we see in His hand
> The print of the nail that marred it,
> Except we see in His side
> The mark of the spear that scarred it,
> We are right to refuse to believe,
> To challenge His claims and doubt them,
> For the wounds are the sign of the Christ
> And He will not come without them.

The closing verse of that poem brings one to the fact that it is not enough simply to assert that you believe in the Atonement. There must be personal appropriation of the purchase of the Crucified One. Her last stanza reads:

> For it is not enough for our faith
> That others have seen and known Him;
> But each for himself must see,
> And each for himself must own Him;
> And each must touch the print of the nails,
> The proof of His claim receiving.
> And each must cry, 'My Lord, my God',
> And fall at His feet, believing.

But one of her most striking testimonies to the Cross is found in her Nature Psalms, her little booklet, "Out of Doors." She laid hold of a report concerning a beautiful natural formation of the Cross on the Island of Manan, in the Bay of Fundy. We have since received a photograph of that very rock. With the mental picture of that rocky Cross before her keen vision, she penned her lines on "The Crag of the Cross." It is one of her longest poems. Listen to the first stanza:

> Beside the bleak coast of the Northland,
> Where winds with the tempests keep tryst,
> Amid a wild welter of waters,
> An island looms out of the mist;
> Forever the high tide of Fundy
> Sweeps past with a rush and a roar,
> Forever the gulls cry their warning
> When fog wreathes the desolate shore;
> Above the gray billows the cliffs frown,
> Above the grim cliffs bends the sky,
> And clear against cliff-side and heavens
> The Crag of the Cross rises high.

Her second stanza may well be included here:

> Of old hath He laid its foundation
> Who holdeth the sea in His hand,
> Who weigheth its waters by measure
> And setteth their bounds by the sand;
> And slowly His craftsmen have carved it,
> The frost and the storm and the wave
> Rough-hewn from the rock everlasting
> Where aeons their annals might grave.
> Long, long, ere o'er Bethlehem's manger
> The Star shed its radiant light,
> And long ere on Calvary's summit
> The noonday was shrouded in night;
> While kingdoms and nations had risen
> And played their brief parts for a day,
> And countless new creeds and old systems
> Had flourished and passed to decay;
> While oracles lapsed into silence
> And prophets grew weary and dumb,
> The Cross, through the centuries waiting,
> Was pledge of a faith yet to come.

That poem in its entirety must surely be one of the things that will remain as her contribution to the English language, and to the Christian faith. When one comes to the next item of Christian faith and reaches the theme of the Resurrection rich inspiration flows from her pen. It was not just to supply the demand for Easter cards. Her heart welled up in fellowship with a living Saviour. In one poem already quoted "I Know", she has a resurrection verse as follows:

> 'I know' - upon this lighthouse tower
> The winds and waves shall beat in vain;
> I know that my Redeemer lives
> And in His death all Death was slain;
> I know my life is hid with Him
> Beyond the reach of change or harm,
> And life and death to me are one
> Within the shelter of His arm.

Another resurrection poem she took from the little word in Matthew 28:6, "He is risen, as He said." The last three words were her title. It ran as follows:

> He has risen, as He said.
> Christ the Lord the promise gave
> To His weak disciples' hearts
> When He told of cross and grave;
> But they failed to understand
> And they heard - or heeded - not,
> And, when they had seen Him dead
> All His promise they forgot.
> "So upon that Easter morn
> When the long, sad hours were past,
> And they came unto the tomb
> Where the watch had sealed Him fast,
> They had not remembered yet
> All the gracious words He said,
> Till the shining angel spake:
> 'He is risen, as He said.'

Two other stanzas complete her resurrection poem, and lead on to the truth that should always follow, the Blessed Hope of the Christian.

Her conversion in the Methodist Church, even though she had been reared in the midst of Baptists, gave no predisposition to stress the doctrine of the Second Advent. Methodists have largely suppressed that truth since the days of the Wesleys and Coke, and yet her faith here came from the simple Word of God. She could not sit and listen to her Lord as He said, "If I go away, I will come again," without simply asking what He meant. And when she followed on through the great scene of His glorious ascension and listened to the men in white, she thought she had her answer. "This same Jesus, whom ye have seen go from you into Heaven, shall so come in like manner as you have seen Him go." So she turned her pen from time to time to that which was to her a comforting hope. Laying hold of the words of the loved Disciple, "We Shall See Him As He Is," she wrote the simple stanzas:

> We shall see Him as He is
> Not as men for long have thought Him,
> While through all the circling years
> Blind and stumbling they have sought Him;
> Not as fierce and warring sects
> Each in turn have claimed to know Him,
> Nor as Love, who knoweth yet
> But in part, is fain to show Him.
> Nor as even Hope, who far
> In the country of her dreaming,
> Hath espied Him, like a star
> Faintly through the shadows gleaming.

> Nor as Faith in visions fair
> From her mountain height hath seen Him,
> Darkly through the glass of time,
> With the mists of earth to screen Him.

> We shall see Him as He is
> Face to face shall we behold Him,
> When the visions and the dreams
> And the clouds no more enfold Him;
> In His likeness we shall wake,
> Spirit unto spirit calling,
> 'Neath the white flame of His eyes
> All the earthly from us falling;
> We shall stand all spotless, pure,
> Gazing on His unveiled graces,
> While we feel the glory grow
> On our rapt and upturned faces.
> Till the Master, looking down,
> On the silver of His fining,
> Shall behold reflected there
> His own image clear and shining.

That Blessed Hope spurred her to missionary activity. She sought to do her part in hastening the coming of the Lord by encouraging in every way she could the spread of the Gospel in all lands. She expressed her hope of the glorious day when the Gospel and the Christ should prevail, in the words of the poem she entitled, "As the Waters Cover the Sea." But one other of her best poems on the Second Coming she took from the word of the great Resurrection chapter, "We shall not all sleep but we shall all be changed"; and in 1 Thessalonians 4:17: "We shall be caught up … to meet the Lord in the air." That Blessed Hope caught her up in the muse of the poet, and she penned the words:

> We shall change –
> Into something new and strange.
> Death shall set his captives free;
> Mortal shall immortal be;
> We shall put the earthly by
> Sin and sin's defiling stain,
> Weakness, weariness, and pain
> Evermore like Him to be
> Whom at last our eyes shall see;
> Into something fair and strange
> We shall change.
>
> We shall go –
> Not with funeral cortege slow,
> Not with toll of passing bell
> Human grief and gloom to tell,
> But with shout of Christ on high,
> Trump of God and angel's cry;
> We who dwell as exiles here,
> Longing for a land more dear,
> Joyful, to our home above,
> Joyful, to the Lord we love,
> From all evils here below
> We shall go.

She took no interest in hair-splitting theories about the Second Coming. She deprecated controversy and bitterness in this sphere. She fellowshipped and loved all those who love His appearing. This was no doctrine with her. She was looking for a Person who had given a promise. When she saw earth's woes, she longed for the coming again of the World's Redeemer.

9

Songs of Comfort

It was not in the setting forth of Christian doctrine in poetic form that Annie Johnson Flint's greatest ministry lay – it was in the application of Christian truths to the experiences of life. It was to the weary pilgrim on life's journey that she sang her sweetest song. She knew the One who was the Man of Sorrows. She had drunk her own cup of bitterness and could sympathize. And to the weary traveller along earth's way she sought to sing her songs of help and hope. One of the sweetest single stanza poems that she wrote was perhaps "Thy Strength and My Day":

> Give me Thy strength for my day, Lord,
> That wheresoe'er I go,
> There shall no danger daunt me
> And I shall fear no foe;
> So shall no task o'ercome me,
> So shall no trial fret,
> So shall I walk unwearied
> The path where my feet are· set;

> So shall I find no burden
> Greater than I can bear,
> So shall I have a courage
> Equal to all my care;
> So shall no grief o'erwhelm me,
> So shall no wave o'erflow;
> Give me Thy strength for my day, Lord,
> Cover my weakness so.

We wonder if anyone, outside of sacred writ, ever met the weary pilgrim with a sweeter word than that which Annie Johnson Flint incorporated into her little poem on "The Court of the King'. The opening stanzas read:

> With staff that had failed in my need
> Where the road had been stony and steep;
> With lamp that was smoking and dim;
> Though the darkness was growing more deep;
> Weary, too weary to pray
> And too heavy-hearted to sing,
> Faint with the toils of the way
> I came to the court of the King.

> There where the fountains fall cool,
> Their waters unfailing and pure;
> There where the ministering palms
> Stand like His promises sure,
> Oh! there was peace in its shade,
> Oh! there was rest in its calm;
> And its sweet silences lay
> On my bruised spirit like balm.

Surely, weary pilgrim on Life's journey, this woman must have been in one of Bunyan's pilgrim parties. She knew the things that you and I have passed by the way, when she. wrote the above sweet words. And then she went on to say:

> Long did I kneel in His court,
> And walk in his garden so fair;
> All I had lost or had lacked
> I found in His treasuries there;
> Oil to replenish my lamp,
> His kindness a crown for my head,
> For the staff that had wounded my hand
> The rod of His mercy instead.

With scarcely a break in the stanzas she continues on to its conclusion:

> A garment of praises I found
> For the sullen, dark garb I had worn,
> And sandals of peace for the feet
> That the rocks and the briers had torn;
> Joy for my mourning He gave,
> Making my Spirit to sing,
> And, girded with gladness and strength,
> I passed from the court of the King.

Only one who had borne the heat and burden of the day; only one who had shared earth's trials and been through earth's tumult, and then turned to the quietness of the closet and to the treasures of the precious Word of God, could have penned such lines as those. We question whether a pain-free life could ever have beaten out the treasures that she has left for our enjoyment. The writer of these lines has again and again picked up one of her little poem pamphlets in times of discouragement and the words have faced him with cheer and help, and he has longed that others might read that which blessed his soul. Take such a one as she put forth under the title, "Your Father Knoweth":

> He knoweth the need of my life
> For shelter and raiment and food;
> In each trifling care of the day
> The word of His promise is good ;
> He knoweth my thought from afar,
> The wish that I never have told,
> And every unspoken desire
> His wisdom doth grant or withhold.

Then come two other stanzas, one of which is headed "He knoweth the way that I take," and the third stanza, "He knoweth the need of my soul." And then she comes to the concluding verse in the sweet words:

> He knoweth me – yet He can love,
> Can wait with love's patience divine, ·
> My stubborn and arrogant heart
> Its will to His own to resign;
> He knoweth my frame is but dust;
> He knoweth how much it can bear;
> I rest in that knowledge supreme;
> I trust in His power and care.

In those more than forty years of suffering there was many a day which would have pressed out from the poet's heart the words that we have in another sweet song:

> I am so tired, Lord – oh, lift me up
> To Thine unfailing strength and rest me so.
> I am so weary of the stress and strain,
> The fevered rush, the grinding daily toil
> For daily bread, that wears my poor life out
> To keep life in – oh, lift me, lift me, Lord,
> To Thine enfolding peace, and calm me so.

And that poem leads through and on and up until this last word which evidences that the answer to her wish and her cry had come: "What need have I of any more than this?" We do not wonder that her little book entitled "Songs of Faith and Comfort", from which this gem is taken has been passed on to thousands of those who are treading a similar path. Annie Johnson Flint believed in and exemplified what some have called the "deeper life" and others designate "the higher life." She believed that Christians should go on, ever on, experimentally into the truth of God. Taking the words of Paul, "Therefore, leaving the first principles let us go on unto perfection" she wrote a poetic incitement under the title, "Let Us Go On":

> Some of us stay at the cross,
> Some of us wait at the tomb,
> Quickened and raised together with Christ,
> Yet lingering still in its gloom;
> Some of us bide at the Passover feast
> With Pentecost all unknown –
> The triumphs of grace in the heavenly place

That our Lord has made our own.

If the Christ who died had stopped at the cross
His work had been incomplete,
If the Christ who was buried had stayed in the tomb
He had only known defeat;
But the Way of the Cross never stops at the Cross,
And the Way of the Tomb leads on,
To victorious grace in the heavenly place.
Where the risen Lord has gone.

So, let us go on with our Lord
To the fulness of God He has bought,
Unsearchable riches of glory and good
Exceeding our uttermost thought;
Let us grow up into Christ,
Claiming His life and its powers,
The triumphs of grace in the heavenly place
That our conquering Lord has made ours.

Annie Johnson Flint has taught us the lesson once more that the deepest things are often comprehended by the simple mind, and that the things profound can be apprehended by the child. The highest heights and the deepest depths she expressed in such sweet language, and language that can be understood by all. So many of her best poems found their suggestions from the texts which she heard and read. The sermon took a simpler form when she put it forth in rhyme. We think any preacher can preach the better from Ephesians 3:17-19, "That we may be able to comprehend the breadth and length depth and height and to know the love of Christ which passeth knowledge," after reading her poetic homily. Her little sermonette takes up in its five stanzas, five great questions from the text. It starts off:

> How broad is His love?
> Oh, as broad as man's trespass,
> As wide the need of the world can be;
> And yet for the need of one soul it can narrow
> He came to the world and He came to me.

Under her first heading she comprehends as much as many a preacher gets into a whole sermon. Then take her second stanza, which takes up the question of dimension:

> How long is His love?
> Without end or beginning,
> Eternal as Christ and His life it must be,
> For, to everlasting as from everlasting
> He loveth the world and He loveth me.

She gathers up the ends of the two eternities of the past and future and packs them all into that little verse expressive of the love of Christ. And then she continues:

> How deep is His love?
> Oh, as deep as man's sinning,
> As low as that uttermost vileness can be;
> In the fathomless gulf of the Father's forsaking
> He died for the world and He died for me.

In those four simple lines she takes one to Calvary and the great theme in which the Christ Himself cries out that tremendous question, "My God! My God! why hast Thou forsaken me?" And she makes that the plumbline to try and fathom its depths. What will she do with the other dimension? You get it in her fourth stanza:

> How high is His love?
> It is high as the heavens,
> As high as the throne of His glory must be;
> And yet from that height He hath stooped to redeem us,
> He so loved the world and He so loved me.

She passes from dimensions to comprehension, and in her closing verse she presses home that love into the bounds of personal experience where she raises in the final stanza the last question:

> How great is His love?
> Oh, it passeth all knowledge,
> No man's comprehension its measure can be;
> It filleth the world, yet each heart may contain it
> He so loved the world and he so loves me.

We challenge Christians to pick up any one of her little booklets without finding something that will call their lives to deeper trust in Christ, or make the presence of the Christ more real to the daily life. In this brief sketch we cannot quote more largely than we have done.

10

Sunset and Eventide

Miss Flint determined that there was to be "no moaning of the bar when she put out to sea." The last years of her life brought her no ease from her affliction, no lessening of the pain and suffering. And yet, we think that in those closing years she really exemplified more than ever some of the sweetness of her earlier verses. Her "Water Lily Story" was one of the first poems in print, and we like to think of it as typical of her life. It was really written for a baby book in July. She was moved to write it in a way that turned out to be a real providence for her. She had faced an unexpected deficit in her income. When this poem was offered to the "Youths' Companion" it found a response and brought her a cheque that just met her need. Again it takes us back to her girlhood observations. We wish we could present "The Water Lily", as she wrote it:

> When first I woke to life;
> Deep down in the river's bed,
> I could not breathe for the stifling ooze

> And the blackness over my head.
> In darkness I longed for the light,
> Prisoned, I yearned to be free,
> In dreams I pined for the sky and the wind,
> For star and bird and tree;
> And I said: 'I will rise to that upper air,
> And the life that draweth me.'
> The twining weeds of the water-world
> Reached out and held me fast;
> The lithe reeds wove a tangled net
> To catch me as I passed;
> The creeping things of mire and mud
> Beckoned and bade me stay;
> In the treacherous current, swift and strong,
> I felt my weak stem sway;
> But through them, over them, past them all,
> I took my upward way.

Then one thinks of the closing part of this wonderful life as it seemed to open up and bloom for the world's blessing, and she goes on:

> Till, white, white,
> Brimmed with sunshine and steeped in light,
> I lifted up my fragrant cup -
> Bloom of the daytime and star of the night
> In rapture I gazed at the heavens blue
> And knew that all my dreams were true.

In the last stanza she concludes with the words :

> Till, pure and white,
> Filled with glory and steeped in light,
> No trace of the soil from whence it springs
> Staining the Soul's expanding wings,
> You too shall see the arching heaven's blue
> And find that all your dreams are true.
> You shall eat of joy as your daily bread,
> Through love you shall learn and by loving live;
> You shall drink of life at the fountain head,
> And that life to the world in sweetness give.

In later years, her Water Lily poem was broadcast from a San Francisco station and brought her a great response and dozens of letters. In Miss Flint's own notes from which this sketch of her life is written, her affliction receives little notice. She would have it so. Although crippled, she did not consider herself helpless in the sense that she could do nothing but bemoan her lot. She believed that God had laid her aside for a purpose, even although that purpose was obscured to her at times, but she also believed that He had work for her to do, and she put her very best into the writing of her poems, rendering this ministry unto Him.

The result has been that her verses have an unusually deep appeal to human hearts. The simple reason is that she felt what she wrote, and out of the crucible of suffering she was able to administer that comfort to others wherewith she herself had been comforted of God. No one but God and she knew what suffering she endured as the disease became worse with the passing of the years, and new complications developed. But through it all, her faith in the goodness and mercy of God never wavered. There were many times no doubt when her soul would be burdened with the mystery of it all and the why and wherefore of the thing she was called upon to endure.

In that respect she was most human like the rest of us, but the marvellous thing is that her faith never faltered, and that she was at all times able to say "Thy Will be Done." For more than forty years there was hardly a day when she did not suffer pain. For thirty-seven years she had become increasingly helpless. Every joint in her body had become rigid, although she was able to turn her head, and in great pain write a few lines on paper. But long before these later years of helplessness she had received her one great affirmation from God which settled all her doubts. Perhaps the shortest stanza which she wrote was upon the words, "Wherefore all the promises of God in Him are yea and amen." To this verse she wrote:

'Is God–?' 'Hath God–?' 'Doth God–?'
Man's 'Why?' and How?'
In ceaseless iteration storm the sky.
'I am'; 'I will'; 'I do'; sure Word of God, Yea and Amen,
Christ answereth each cry;
To all our anguished questionings and doubts
Eternal affirmation and reply.

In less than a week before the passing, Mrs. Bingham and Mr. Stock, with whom Miss Flint had had most of the correspondence about the publication of her poems, called to see her, in the early morning. The nurse gave her "no" to the request for an interview, but when the name was passed in, she said it mattered not whether it was morning, noon or night, nothing should keep them out of her chamber. And for an hour they had delightful fellowship. There was no thought then of the immediate passing. But on the Thursday morning, the following week, September 8th, she felt very tired and wondered if she could live the day out. When the doctor was called he stated that it was just weakness. But all that day she did not improve and the doctor was called again in the evening. He saw at once that she was in great distress and her heart was behaving badly.

Before giving her a hypodermic he asked if there was anything she wished to say or have her friends do as she might not rally. Her last words were: "I have nothing to say. It's all right." A few minutes later she had gone to be with Christ. Sorrow, affliction, pain, suffering and death was ended forever, for the former things had passed away. One may well apply to her end the words of the book of Revelation: "These are they which came out of great tribulation and have washed their robes and have made them white in the blood of the Lamb." And going to another book of a great dreamer and writer of whom Miss Flint was very fond, we have drawn forth the words that told the story in a similar fashion:

> *"Now the day drew on when she must be gone. And behold all the Banks beyond the River were full of horses and chariots which were coming down from above to accompany her to the City gates. So she came forth and entered the River with a beck and a farewell to those that followed her to the River side. The last words she was heard to say here were 'I come, Lord, to be with Thee and bless Thee.'"*

In considering the life of Annie Johnson Flint one is perplexed with questions as old as humanity itself, such as the mystery of pain and suffering. That the wicked should suffer as the reward for their wrong-doing seems only just and right, but that the righteous should have to pass through the furnace sometimes heated seven times is a great stumbling block to many people. That is because we only see half the circle of life. One thing we are sure of, and that is that the Divine Potter makes no mistakes as He molds the clay left unresisting in His hands. "When it had come forth from his hand, he had fashioned it indeed, a goodly vessel prepared and fit for the Master's use." Miss Flint's beautiful poem on the Potter would make a fitting conclusion to this life, the second verse of which reads:

> The Potter fashioned the Cup
> With whirling wheel and hand;
> Hour by hour He built it up
> To the form that His thought had planned.
> 'Twas broken, and broken again,
> Marred by a flaw, a crack, a stain,
> Marred, so he made it again - and again;
> Shaped it from laughter and labor and pain,
> From hopes that withered and hopes fulfilled,
> From dreams forgotten and longings stilled;
> From rose and thorn and the gold of morn,
> From dark and bright and the stars of night,
> From joy and beauty and all delight;
> From flower and weed, from root and seed,
> From bird and river and tossing tree;
> From wind and fire and heart's desire,
> The pearl and the shell and the foam o' the sea;

> From the years that were and the years to be;
> And the Cup that He fashioned He gave to me.

And then she gives the purpose of the fashioning of the Cup. No one can read it without thinking of this life and its accomplishments. Surely the vessel was what God intended it to be. That vessel was to hold and to pour out the rivers of living water and truly Annie Johnson Flint has done this. And the closing stanza continues:

> And the clay is Thine, O Potter, Thine;
> But the cup of life Thou hast made is mine
> To save or lose, to waste or use,
> For a poison drink or a draught divine;
> To hold it lightly and fling it away,
> Or give it for service every day;
> To leave it an empty and useless thing
> Or fill with the glory of ministering;
> The word of cheer and the kindly deed
> For passing pilgrim or childish need,
> Thy tender thought by suffering taught,
> With comfort and healing and power fraught,
> To lift and strengthen and help and bless
> The souls in sorrow and loneliness;
> The loving touch that means so much,
> The smile and the look of sympathy.
> With these shall I fill this gift to me,
> Fill to the brim and running o'er,
> And into the world its treasure pour,
> Yet, giving ever, shall have the more,
> And through the nights and through the days

I drink to His praise – to the Potter's praise
Who gave the cup to me.

More by Annie Johnson Flint

He Giveth More Grace: One Hundred Poems by Annie Johnson Flint

This collection of one hundred of her poems contains Annie's most well-known writings, as well many of the lesser-known ones. Many of them reflect an unwavering faith in her God and His promises, and a belief that He was always with her and supporting her and had a plan for her life, even though her way might be hard and she couldn't currently see what his purposes for her might be. Her unwavering reliance on God's grace to cope with trials on a daily basis is also very evident, as is her deep love for her Saviour, Jesus Christ. What also shines through many of her poems is a love of God's creation, and this fact is made all the more remarkable because her arthritis would have prevented her from exploring so much of it.

God Hath Not Promised - One Hundred More Poems by Annie Johnson Flint

Following on from the best-selling first volume of Annie Johnson Flint's poems is a second volume of 100 poems, written with the same matchless skill and impactful craft.

Grace Sufficient - One Hundred Further Poems by Annie Johnson Flint

Ravi Zacharias has described Annie Johnson Flint as one of the greatest hymnwriters, and this third volume of 100 of Annie's poems serves to provide additional evidence to support his claim. Like the other volumes, these poems primarily focus on the return of the Lord Jesus, the wonder and beauty of nature, and the trusting of God through the trials of life, including pain and bereavement.

More From Hayden Press

100 Hymns and Poems of Love and Devotion

This book comprises 100 hymns and poems that each express love and devotion to the Lord Jesus or to God the Father, with contributions from writers such as Charles Wesley, Daniel Webster Whittle, Horatius Bonar, J.N. Darby, C.H. Gabriel, Annie Johnson Flint, P.P. Bliss, Frances Ridley Havergal and Fanny J. Crosby. Also included are biographies of 17 of the authors.

The Life and Life-Work of P.P. Bliss - A Biography

P.P. Bliss was one of the most gifted hymn-writers and composers of the late Victorian era, known for hymns such as Man of Sorrows, Dare to be a Daniel, I Will Sing of My Redeemer, Ho! My Comrades, See the Signal, Brightly Beams Our Father's Mercy and More Holiness Give Me. As this fascinating biography records, Bliss's life was tragically cut short, but not before he had left a legacy that is a source of joy and encouragement to millions of Christians today.

Manufactured by Amazon.ca
Acheson, AB